If I Was a ~~Good Doctor~~ Handbook of Sleepless Nights, Endless Charts, and Pretending Coffee Is a Balanced Diet

Simple, sarcasm-inspired guidance for everyday life

by
Gordon Murray

If I Was a Good Doctor: A Handbook of
Sleepless Nights, Endless Charts, and
Pretending Coffee Is a Balanced Diet
© 2025 by Gordon Murray

I'd embrace my seventh consecutive night shift, because who needs a functional circadian rhythm when you can have fluorescent lighting and the musical hum of IV pumps serenading your soul.

Medical literature suggests sleep is important, but if I was a good doctor, I'd instead be a staunch advocate for the "sleep when you retire" doctrine, fueled solely by vending machine cuisine and wishful thinking.

Example: At 3:12 a.m., I diagnose myself with déjà vu when the same nurse asks for antibiotic orders for the fourth time, but I'm too sleep-deprived to remember if I've already approved them.

I would savor my eleventh cup of coffee instead of lunch, because nothing says "nutritional balance" like jittery hands and a heart rate rivalling the monitor alarms.

While most people count calories, I count milligrams of caffeine and minutes until my next bathroom break, which doubles as my only exercise and my chance to practice mindful breathing in a locked stall.

Example: My lunch break is rescheduled for the ninth time, so I settle for powdered creamer and a granola bar I found in my white coat from last February.

I'd write twenty chart notes per patient, because if I was a good doctor, I'd treat the electronic medical record like my own private diary—minus the secrets and with more risk of being audited.

I remind myself that every moment spent charting is a moment not spent making questionable small talk, and besides, who needs memorable patient interactions when you can immortalize your feelings in templated phrases?

Example: After a twelve-hour shift, my documentation time rivals my clinical hours, and I still forget to press "save," losing four pages of soul-baring narrative on a ruptured appendix.

I'd ignore my friends' beach trip invitations, since as a good doctor, I prefer the refreshing sting of hand sanitizer and the soothing caress of an N95 mask to the gentle touch of ocean breezes.

Sunburn is overrated, and anyway, nothing builds camaraderie like the communal suffering of a call room without windows, where tan lines are but a distant memory reserved for those who know what "weekend" means.

Example: While my friends post sun-drenched selfies, I'm monitoring potassium levels and watching the sun set through a supply closet window, clutching a pager as my only accessory.

I would perfect the art of pretending to remember every patient's name, because clearly, my memory is a steel trap and not a sieve worn out by 36-hour shifts and identical hospital gowns.

The look of heartfelt recognition works wonders, even when I'm silently praying their chart loads faster than the awkward silence grows; if patients can fake remembering me, it's only fair I reciprocate.

Example: Called urgently to see "Mr. White," I confidently greet the wrong family, only realizing my mistake when they introduce themselves and I pretend it was a "routine cross-check."

I'd master the fine art of charting patient notes at 3 a.m. instead of, say, actually getting any sleep or dreaming of a life outside the hospital walls.

They say documentation is key, so naturally, prioritizing endless charts over REM cycles is the hallmark of any good doctor—or at least any doctor with carpal tunnel and perpetual eye bags.

Example: After a 14-hour shift, I'd carefully record every medication change while trying to remember if I actually prescribed them or merely hallucinated it during my fifth coffee.

I'd develop a taste for stale vending machine dinners, since apparently, haute cuisine in medicine means anything with a sell-by date in this decade.

Balanced nutrition is vital for peak performance, and nothing says "fit for work" like a dinner of neon-orange chips and mystery meat, washed down with lukewarm diet soda.

Example: My colleagues enjoy sushi takeout, while I'd savor a tepid chicken sandwich from the vending machine, peeling off the plastic and pretending it's tapas.

I'd perfect smiling sincerely at 6 a.m. rounds, instead of screaming internally after being woken up every hour on the hour by alarms and pages.

Maintaining a positive bedside manner is crucial; showing any trace of existential dread or sleep deprivation might lower patient morale—even if it's the honest, human response.

Example: I'd nod cheerfully at the chief resident, clutching my fourth cup of coffee and pretending I didn't just nap upright in the supply closet.

I'd attend mandatory "wellness" seminars about work-life balance during my only free lunch, instead of, say, spending ten uninterrupted minutes eating or contemplating my existence.

Wellness is important, so nothing boosts morale like hearing about yoga and mindfulness while shoveling a granola bar and drafting discharge summaries between bites.

Example: *I'd sit in a windowless conference room, nodding through PowerPoint slides about "personal boundaries," while paging through lab results on my phone under the table.*

I'd memorize the intricate art of apologizing for being late to everything outside the hospital, since apparently, "saving lives" doesn't count as a valid excuse to friends or family.

Social obligations don't pause for call schedules, so crafting the perfect apology for missing birthdays, anniversaries, or any event with actual joy is an essential skill.

Example: I'd text apologies from the call room, still in scrubs, as the family dinner I was supposed to attend starts without me—again.

I'd remember to eat lunch before 6 p.m., if I wasn't so busy treating everyone else's indigestion while mine matured into a complex philosophical crisis.

After all, skipping meals is clearly the best way to empathize with patients who can't keep anything down, and my stomach's growling just adds a dramatic soundtrack to my patient notes.

Example: *By the time I unwrap my sad granola bar, the cafeteria is closed, but at least the vending machine whispers sweet nothings of empty calories at 9:17 p.m.*

I would definitely keep my handwriting legible, but I like giving pharmacists a little mystery in their day—makes life spicy for everyone involved.

Illegible scrawls aren't a flaw; they're a rite of passage, a shared puzzle that unites the medical community in mutual confusion and collective hope for the correct medication.

Example: *After three calls from the pharmacy, my "metformin" is finally deciphered—on the fourth suggestion, which is honestly better odds than my college Latin quizzes.*

I'd go home after my shift ends, if my patients' crises respected the concept of time as much as my phone company does when billing my overtime minutes.

The hospital clock is just a decorative suggestion, and I find that every "quick check" on a patient usually turns into an all-night camping trip in scrubs.

Example: I pack up at 7, only to be paged for a "minor" issue—five hours, zero dinner, and one fresh admission later, my bag is still under my desk.

I'd treat my own cold with actual medication, but self-diagnosing with denial and a double espresso is basically the gold standard of doctor wellness.

Why use evidence-based medicine on myself when I can ignore symptoms until they either disappear or become a dazzling teaching opportunity for interns?

Example: *Midway through rounds, I cough up a lung, assure the team it's "allergies," and mainline caffeine until my immune system files for bankruptcy.*

I'd enjoy weekends like normal people, but honestly, nothing says "leisure" like catching up on paperwork in a windowless office while everyone else is at brunch.

Sacrificing Saturday sunlight is practically a doctor's spa ritual, except instead of cucumber water I get highlighters, and instead of relaxation I get the thrill of chasing missing signatures.

Example: My friends post mimosas on social media, while I rediscover last month's patient forms and develop a meaningful relationship with my office chair.

I'd gladly swap my entire weekend for a chance to write progress notes so detailed that even the patient's goldfish would feel represented in the record.

There's nothing quite as satisfying as knowing that while everyone else is at brunch, I'm documenting bowel movements with such flourish that a Pulitzer nomination feels imminent. After all, accuracy is the true breakfast of champions.

Example: Instead of my cousin's wedding, I spent my Saturday night meticulously describing the subtle nuances of a dressing change in the EMR, accompanied only by the distant hum of a janitor's vacuum.

I'd choose to measure urine output over sleeping eight consecutive hours, because dreams can't be charted and nobody ever paged me for REM cycles.

Sleep is overrated anyway—what truly matters is the hourly assurance that kidneys are still working. Besides, who needs rest when you can have the thrill of a 3 a.m. fluid assessment?

Example: *While my friends compared sleep apps, I set my alarm to check a Foley bag at intervals, perfecting the art of tiptoeing past sleeping patients with the grace of a caffeinated ninja.*

I'd volunteer to eat exclusively from the hospital vending machine for a week, just to experience the culinary adventure of room-temperature chicken salad and inspirational granola bars.

Gourmet cuisine is wasted on people who don't appreciate the nuanced flavors of pre-packaged sodium bombs. Sacrificing nutrition is a small price for the privilege of not leaving the hospital for days.

Example: As my roommate posted Instagram stories from a Michelin-starred bistro, I debated if the "tuna surprise" was worth the risk or if I should stick to a tried-and-true packet of stale cheese crackers.

I'd rather spend my birthday learning the subtle art of deciphering illegible consult notes than blowing out candles anywhere outside a supply closet.

The thrill of solving cryptic penmanship trumps any party game, and presents can't compare to the satisfaction of finally guessing that "q2h" was really "q4h" all along.

Example: My big day featured a celebratory hunt for the one resident whose handwriting looked like hieroglyphics, followed by a slice of leftover sheet cake balanced precariously atop a stack of discharge summaries.

I'd forgo any actual vacation just for the chance to be on call and respond to pages that are 90% about typos, 10% about real emergencies.

Who wants white sand beaches when you could have the soothing glow of a pager at 2 a.m.? The tropical breeze is nothing compared to the adrenaline rush of "STAT" requests for a missing allergy update.

Example: Instead of sipping cocktails by the pool, I spent my "time off" clarifying that yes, acetaminophen and paracetamol are, in fact, the same thing—for the third time that night.

I'd happily trade my weekend getaway for another 48-hour shift, because who needs beaches when you have fluorescent lights and the soothing beep of a heart monitor.

Studies show vitamin D is overrated, especially compared to the invigorating glow of hospital corridors and the distant screams of malfunctioning pagers. Besides, sunburns are avoidable if you never see the sun.

Example: *While friends posted photos from a mountain hike, I was knee-deep in admission notes, discovering that my only hike was sprinting between the ER and the ICU for twelve hours straight.*

I'd forgo a home-cooked meal for a lukewarm vending machine burrito at 3 a.m., because fine dining is all about ambiance—and nothing beats the aroma of disinfectant and last Tuesday's coffee.

The culinary arts are wasted on doctors, whose palates are expertly trained to distinguish between different brands of instant ramen. Gourmet cuisine is best experienced in five-minute increments between code blues.

Example: As my partner sent photos of their pasta night, I savored microwave nachos that fused themselves to the plate, delicately garnished with the lingering taste of latex gloves.

I would gladly cancel my own doctor's appointment so I can spend the afternoon convincing patients that, yes, they really should keep theirs.

Preventive care for myself is unnecessary when I have WebMD and a robust sense of denial. Much better to focus on ensuring my patients don't follow my example.

Example: *I rescheduled my annual checkup for the fourth time to cover a colleague's clinic, only to spend the day phoning patients who were "too busy" to come in.*

I'd sacrifice eight hours of uninterrupted sleep for the privilege of being startled awake by a 2 a.m. call about Tylenol dosing, because rest is overrated when you can operate in a perpetual fugue.

Sleep hygiene is for amateurs; professionals thrive on adrenaline and questionable decisions made in the twilight hours. My circadian rhythm closely resembles a toddler's after a candy binge.

Example: *Just as my head hit the pillow, my pager serenaded me with a consult about a patient's mild headache, which I addressed through eyes half-closed and a brain running on autopilot.*

I would much rather memorize 47 new passwords for electronic medical records than remember my own Netflix login, since entertainment is less critical than seamless documentation and maximum security.

Cybersecurity is paramount, especially when it means spending your lunch break resetting passwords and cursing two-factor authentication. Personal accounts can wait; progress notes cannot.

Example: I spent twenty minutes wrestling with login screens before accessing a chart, while my streaming account locked me out for inactivity—an apt metaphor for my social life.

I'd recommend swapping out all personal relationships for a stable Wi-Fi connection and an emotional attachment to my pager, given their superior reliability and lower risk of sudden disappointment.

Patients and paperwork never ghost me, unlike my friends who've forgotten what I look like without a stethoscope. At this point, my healthiest relationship is with the hospital's vending machine.

Example: I missed my best friend's wedding because I was on call, but at least my pager and I shared a romantic dinner of cold instant noodles in the break room.

To be a good doctor, I'd consider six hours of sleep per week a luxury, not a right, since dreaming about patient charts is basically multitasking.

Sleep is for people who don't have 27 unread patient messages and a caffeine tolerance that rivals their student debt. Besides, nothing says "alert and focused" like involuntary eyelid twitches.

Example: After a 28-hour shift, I once tried to clock out of the hospital using my coffee mug, which, to be fair, saw me more often than my own bed.

I would wholeheartedly suggest replacing all meals with intravenous coffee, since chewing just gets in the way of reviewing lab results and developing a mild caffeine-induced existential crisis.

Proper nutrition is aspirational, but liquid calories are efficient and pair beautifully with the ambiance of flickering fluorescent lights and the distant sound of code blues.

Example: I regularly eat dinner at 3 a.m.—standing up, over a keyboard—while pretending cold French fries are "deconstructed pommes frites" for culinary morale.

I'd make it a policy to treat every social invitation as a suggestion rather than a commitment, because RSVPing 'maybe' is the most honest diagnosis I can offer these days.

My career gives me the unique ability to disappoint both my mother and my calendar app at the same time. "Flexible scheduling" just means missing every event but catching the flu.

Example: *I RSVP'd to a college reunion eight months in advance but spent the weekend arguing with insurance over a patient's pre-authorization instead of reminiscing over cafeteria pizza.*

If I was a good doctor, I'd master the art of remembering every patient's life story but forgetting where I parked my own car—priorities are priorities.

It's comforting to know that while I might not recall my own PIN, I do have the full medication list of the entire cardiac unit memorized. Personal details are clearly overrated.

Example: I once circled the parking lot for 40 minutes after a shift, only to realize I'd walked to work that morning in a rare moment of optimism.

I'd definitely choose studying medication side effects over remembering what my own friends look like, because in the off chance I see daylight, I need to know which rash is alarming.

Modern medicine expects me to keep a comprehensive mental database of every adverse reaction, but apparently there's no time to maintain basic human relationships, like recognizing my college roommate at the grocery store.

Example: *While diagnosing a patient's hives, I realize I've walked past my lifelong best friend twice in the hospital corridor without a hint of recognition—she thinks I'm giving her the cold shoulder.*

I would always prioritize updating patient charts at 3 a.m. rather than sleeping, since nothing says "good doctor" like meticulously time-stamped notes written in the throes of REM deprivation.

Chart accuracy is paramount, and, after all, the best clinical decisions are made with the cognitive clarity of someone who's been awake since the late Cretaceous period.

Example: *While typing up a medication reconciliation at dawn, I accidentally address the patient as "Mom" and list "caffeine" under both allergies and current medications.*

I'd forgo every hot meal in favor of consuming whatever's left in the vending machine, because gourmet cuisine is for people who aren't busy calculating creatinine clearance on the back of a napkin.

Eating habits become a fascinating experiment in survival, where flavor, nutrient content, and temperature all take a distant backseat to the speed at which I can eat without choking between codes.

Example: I inhale three packs of saltines and a questionable pudding cup for dinner, all while writing discharge summaries on a sticky table in the staff lounge.

I would much rather answer pages about misplaced forms than hear my family singing "Happy Birthday" to my voicemail, because birthdays will always come around, but missing paperwork is apparently a medical emergency.

The hospital operates on the urgent principle that paperwork lost for months becomes a five-alarm blaze the moment I walk away from my phone, outpacing even the most persistent family celebrations.

Example: I step out for a breath of air, and by the time I return, I have five missed calls, three increasingly desperate pages, and a cupcake with a melted candle.

I'd gladly swap any weekend plans for cross-covering three extra services, because the alternative— having an actual social life—might risk the hospital forgetting my existence entirely.

Nothing preserves job security quite like being the only one willing to cancel hiking trips, weddings, and brunches in favor of hunting for consult notes and chasing down elusive radiology reports.

Example: My friends send beach selfies while I spend Saturday night deciphering handwriting that looks like a seismograph mid-earthquake, just to find out if a patient was ever actually seen by cardiology.

I'd gladly swap a hearty meal for cold vending machine crackers at 2 a.m., because culinary excellence peaks when you're hunched over a chart and chewing with one hand.

Nutritional compromise is a small price to pay for patient care, and frankly, gourmet meals are over-rated when compared to the thrill of artificial cheese dust in the ICU.

Example: While friends Instagram tapas, I'm savoring stale saltines in a windowless call room, carefully balancing my dinner and a penlight with equal disappointment.

I'd trade eight hours of restful sleep for one adrenaline-fueled pager symphony, as nothing says 'living the dream' like a 3 a.m. consult interrupting your REM cycle.

Sleep is for amateurs and patients; true professionals operate on the sweet fuel of uncertainty and caffeine withdrawal, perpetually practicing their "startled awake" reflexes.

Example: *My luxury memory foam pillow collects dust while I perfect power-napping upright in a supply closet, stethoscope still hanging from my neck.*

I'd forgo my weekend plans to spend quality time deciphering illegible notes, because nothing brings joy like playing "Guess That Diagnosis" using someone else's creative penmanship.

Social gatherings pale in comparison to the challenge of translating hieroglyphics into actionable care —plus, it builds character and really stretches that medical degree.

Example: While colleagues brunch on patios, I'm squinting at a sticky note scribbled during rounds, praying it wasn't a prescription for "banana, twice daily."

I'd much rather celebrate my birthday with a 12-hour shift and a cupcake smuggled from the nurse's station, since cake tastes best when consumed standing and slightly resentful.

Meaningful milestones are best marked by paging systems and the faint aroma of antiseptic—after all, who needs parties when you have fluorescent lighting and chart audits?

Example: Instead of blowing out candles at home, I'm blowing on microwaved frosting, hoping nobody needs a stat order as I inhale my annual treat in under 60 seconds.

I'd choose answering existential questions from patients' families over my own existential crisis, because nothing soothes the soul like repeated explanations of "rounds" and "test results."

The emotional labor of clarifying the obvious is an unrivaled balm for distraction from self-reflection — plus, it's great practice for pretending you know more than Google.

Example: While friends contemplate the meaning of life, I'm explaining for the fifth time that tea and essential oils do not, in fact, replace antibiotics.

I'd remember my patients' birthdays, allergies, and shoe sizes if only I didn't dedicate every neuron to recalling when I last saw sunlight or my own mailing address.

Prioritizing patient details over personal wellness is a core tenet of good doctoring, or so I assume from my five-minute orientation. If I kept track of my own needs, where would the fun be?

Example: *On rounds, I flawlessly recite a patient's medication history but blank completely when a nurse asks me for my pager number, which I've changed three times to escape notifications.*

I'd savor a leisurely hot meal instead of perfecting the art of scarfing down granola bars in four bites while hiding in a supply closet.

Sustenance is overrated when there are charts to finish and emergencies simmering. Besides, chewing quickly burns more calories and keeps me ready for sprinting to the next code.

Example: My dinner is a lukewarm protein shake sipped between inserting IVs and pretending I don't hear my stomach lamenting the existence of actual food.

I would go home before midnight, but those progress notes aren't going to write themselves, no matter how many times I will them into existence with a blank stare.

Delayed documentation is a rite of passage; the hospital's lights stay on and so, apparently, do I. Sleep, after all, is just an optional continuing education module.

Example: The cleaning crew wishes me a good night as they mop around my desk, and I nod, unsure if the sun has risen or just my caffeine level.

I'd keep my white coat pristine, but I hear coffee stains are now considered a badge of honor and, frankly, the only form of creative expression I have left.

Fashion fades, but the stubborn espresso blot on my pocket is eternal. Why strive for professional polish when everyone can see my true color: "Burnt-Out Beige"?

Example: A colleague asks if I've switched to patterned scrubs, but really, it's just a giant mystery stain and a constellation of pen leaks across my chest.

I would absolutely prioritize my own doctor's appointments, if I didn't believe that self-care is a mythical activity reserved for people who don't know what an EHR login screen looks like.

The best way to empathize with patients is to become one—eventually, when my own symptoms reach the "urgent" threshold or an annual checkup becomes a decades-long milestone.

Example: My phone pings with a reminder for my physical, but it's sandwiched between six consults, two admissions, and whatever fresh chaos is brewing outside my call room.

I'd definitely choose reviewing patient charts at 2 a.m. over sleeping, because who needs REM cycles when you have color-coded folders and the caffeine shakes to keep you warm?

Proper charting is critical for continuity of care and maintaining legal records, or so I'm told in every meeting; besides, dreams are overrated when compared to the thrill of deciphering illegible notes.

Example: Alone in the office, I squint at a smudged prescription while my body wonders why the sun isn't up and my neighbor's dog is probably enjoying my hours in bed.

I would absolutely prefer debating with insurance companies over having an actual lunch break, since gourmet hold music pairs perfectly with the aroma of microwaved leftovers I never get to eat.

Navigating billing codes and coverage denials sharpens my mind and appetite, while skipping meals saves time and maximizes that authentic, fainting-on-the-job experience beloved by medical professionals everywhere.

Example: *After four calls and three policy clarifications, I find my sandwich has fused to the Tupperware, but at least the patient's physical therapy is approved for next year.*

I'd much rather master the art of peering into strangers' throats than attend my own friends' birthday parties, because nothing says "celebration" like comparing tonsils instead of sharing cake.

Social events build relationships, but so does mutual vulnerability under fluorescent exam lights; friendships fade, but the memory of suspicious rashes in hard-to-reach places lingers forever.

Example: *While my friends toast with cocktails and confetti, I'm congratulating a patient for surviving another year without strep—while discreetly checking my calendar for any sign of a party invitation.*

I would happily trade my weekends for on-call shifts, as everyone knows true happiness is a pager's gentle serenade while your family enjoys brunch without you.

Life is all about priorities, and nothing fosters character like missing every leisurely morning for the privilege of diagnosing appendicitis via phone while butter congeals on someone else's croissant.

Example: At 7 a.m. Saturday, I'm triple-checking lab values in the office while texts of pancake stacks and sunny patios roll in from people with time and untroubled digestion.

I'd definitely opt to learn seven EMR systems instead of having a hobby, since nothing relaxes the mind like remembering a new password every 72 hours.

Diversifying my technological frustration portfolio keeps me agile and adaptive, and surely the satisfaction of logging in rivals the fulfillment of painting, gardening, or understanding what "free time" means.

Example: *While my guitar gathers dust, I get to spend quality evenings updating my security questions and hoping "first pet's name" still counts as a valid answer.*

I'd skip my best friend's wedding to finish night rounds on the geriatric floor, because nothing says celebration like tracking bowel movements at 3 a.m. in orthopedic slippers.

Every missed milestone cements my dedication to the craft—or at least that's what I whisper to myself as I sign discharge summaries instead of dancing the cha-cha. Sometimes, sacrifice means watching the livestream on a rolling computer cart.

Example: *Instead of catching the bouquet, I spent my Saturday night checking blood pressure trends and debating whether prune juice counts as aggressive therapy.*

I'd label five-day-old cafeteria sushi as a "nutritional win" and call it dinner, since proper meals are reserved for people who know what lunch breaks feel like.

The food pyramid dissolves into a vague, abstract concept during residency, replaced by the rectangle of a vending machine selection screen. Besides, nothing builds character like culinary roulette with questionable protein.

Example: Staring at a limp rice roll between suture sessions, I convince myself that wasabi packets count as greens and ginger as a balanced side.

I'd enthusiastically volunteer for the 28-hour call shift because apparently, sleep is just a suggestion and heart palpitations are a sign of professional growth.

According to the ancient texts (written by people who hated REM cycles), true commitment means thriving on adrenaline, coffee, and the occasional text from family wondering if I'm still alive.

Example: *After three consecutive codes and twelve cups of coffee, I mistake my own reflection in a window for a new consult.*

I'd keep a signed photo of my bed on the breakroom locker, as a touching reminder of what a full REM cycle might feel like— someday, in a distant, utopian future.

Sentimental tokens help stave off existential dread and foster hope, especially when the only horizontal surface you see all week is a hospital gurney briefly mistaken for home.

Example: I text my pillow goodnight after exam rounds, apologizing for the abandonment, and promise to return by the next blue moon.

I'd treat a successfully microwaved cup of coffee as a personal win, despite the vague taste of burnt plastic and disappointment, because the real caffeine boost comes from shattered expectations.

Hot drinks are a rare luxury in medicine, and temperature is relative: as long as it doesn't solidify on contact with air, it's a five-star experience. Perseverance is measured in sips, not satisfaction.

Example: After reheating the same cup seven times between rapid response calls, I toast to my resilience with a mouthful of tepid, mysterious liquid.

I'd recommend spending every weekend meticulously updating patient charts instead of catching up on sleep or, say, reintroducing myself to the concept of a social life.

After all, nothing screams "living the dream" like color-coding lab results while everyone else is brunching and posting about bottomless mimosas. Prioritizing paperwork over personal sanity is how legends are made.

Example: Last Saturday, while my friends hiked in the sun, I spent hours deciphering handwriting that looked like ancient runes, documenting every potassium level since the dawn of time.

I would suggest skipping actual meals in favor of a well-balanced diet of stale coffee and whatever's left in the vending machine, ideally consumed standing in a supply closet.

The nutritional value of hospital coffee is questionable, but the caffeine content is scientifically proven to prolong consciousness just long enough to finish three more consults. Who needs fiber when you have adrenaline and regret?

Example: *At 3 p.m., I inhaled a bag of pretzels and a lukewarm latte while hiding from the charge nurse behind a pile of IV fluids.*

I'd advocate for answering work emails at 2 a.m., because nothing says "patient-centered care" like insomnia-induced decision-making and autocorrect disasters.

Sleep is for amateurs; true professionals thrive on REM deprivation and existential dread. At a certain point, the difference between your pillow and your laptop blurs anyway.

Example: I once replied to a policy update in the middle of the night and accidentally cc'd the hospital CEO, featuring several creative, sleep-deprived typos.

I would recommend never leaving the hospital before sunset, just to ensure you forget what daylight looks like and maximize your vitamin D deficiency.

The fluorescent lighting in the break room is almost as invigorating as a Mediterranean vacation, plus you don't even have to pack a suitcase—just your emotional baggage.

Example: *When I finally walked to my car at 9 p.m., I was momentarily blinded by the streetlights, having not seen natural light since that brief glimpse through the ambulance bay doors.*

I'd encourage scheduling all personal appointments at 6 a.m., so you can savor the thrill of being both exhausted and late, simultaneously.

There's something uniquely motivating about brushing your teeth in the parking lot and sprinting to morning rounds with a granola bar stuck in your hair. Efficiency is just organized chaos with better time management.

Example: I once had a dentist appointment before my shift and arrived so tired, I nearly asked for a refill on fluoride instead of coffee.

I'd happily exchange eight hours of sleep for eight hours of trying to decipher another doctor's handwriting, because nothing says "medical precision" like a prescription that could double as abstract art.

After all, sleep is overrated when I could spend that time squinting at hieroglyphic chart notes and making wild guesses about patient care. My optometrist appreciates the extra business when my eyesight inevitably fails.

Example: At 2 a.m., I hover over a chart, convinced the previous physician wrote either "metoprolol" or "mop bucket" as the next medication, and I have to make the call.

I'd gladly eat cold cafeteria mystery meat over a hot, home-cooked meal, just to maintain my streak of dining experiences that rival airplane cuisine at 30,000 feet.

Culinary sacrifice builds character and, more importantly, gastrointestinal resilience. Plus, it fosters camaraderie with colleagues who also can't remember what a fresh vegetable tastes like.

Example: My "lunch" is a suspiciously gray chicken patty, consumed standing between two beeping monitors, while coworkers debate whether the sauce is gravy or just a misfire from the condiment pump.

I'd choose to answer pages about Tylenol dosages from three different nurses rather than have an uninterrupted bathroom break, because patient care always comes first—even before basic bodily functions.

Prioritizing others' needs is the hallmark of a good doctor, especially when it means perfecting my bladder control to Olympic level. Hydration is optional; being on call is mandatory.

Example: *Just as I lock the restroom door, my pager erupts with requests for routine orders, ensuring my coffee intake is never fully processed.*

I'd much rather review insurance denials for hours than watch a single episode of a trending TV show, because nothing's more thrilling than the plot twist of "not medically necessary."

Intricate narratives and character development pale in comparison to the suspense of whether an MRI gets approved. Brain teasers are overrated; decoding insurance lingo offers all the mystery I need.

Example: *I spend my evening on hold, listening to smooth jazz while waiting to argue with an insurance rep, missing the season finale everyone will spoil for me tomorrow.*

I'd enthusiastically celebrate special occasions by working a double shift instead of attending family gatherings, because what's a birthday if not another chance to check someone's potassium at midnight?

Traditions are flexible when you're in medicine—who needs cake when you can have vital signs? My loved ones understand that "quality time" means me texting from a call room between emergencies.

Example: I send a quick "happy anniversary" message from the hospital stairwell at 11:54 p.m., just before sprinting to a code blue down the hall.

I'd gladly trade my meticulously crafted sleep schedule for the thrill of deciphering handwriting that even the original author can't interpret, all in the name of patient care.

After all, who needs REM cycles when you can have REM-induced hallucinations while squinting at a scrawled "acetaminophen" that might actually say "appendectomy"? Priorities, like sleep, are overrated in medicine.

Example: I set my alarm for a hopeful six hours, only to spend the night deciphering a resident's chart that references medication instructions written during what had to be a caffeine blackout.

I'd forsake nutritious, home-cooked meals for hospital cafeteria cuisine, because nothing says "medical expertise" like eating a chicken patty that could double as an orthopedic implant.

Meal prepping is a hobby for people with free time and working taste buds, so I prefer my meals tepid, mysterious, and served in a compartmentalized tray with a side of existential dread.

Example: *While reviewing labs at 2 a.m., I grab a "vegetable medley" that suspiciously resembles last week's omelet, but at least it pairs well with my eighth cup of bad coffee.*

I'd pretend my inbox overflowing with administrative emails is a treasure trove of exciting opportunities, rather than a relentless reminder of forms I'll never complete before retirement.

Nothing fuels my passion for medicine like a "mandatory training" email about proper stapler usage, sandwiched between reminders to update my password and invitations to wellness seminars I'll never attend.

Example: I log in for morning rounds, only to be greeted by 37 unread messages, three expired deadlines, and an invitation to a luncheon I'll have to skip for patient admissions.

I'd joyfully hand over my social life to the scheduling gods, confident they know exactly when I should be celebrating major life events — preferably during a 24-hour call shift.

Attending weddings, birthdays, or holidays would only interfere with my true calling: clutching a pager and hoping the code blue is just a test. Besides, there's always next year for fun.

Example: My friends send me party photos while I eat vending machine pretzels in the on-call room, serenaded by the soothing beep of machines and the gentle hum of the fluorescent lights.

I'd enthusiastically embrace presenting at morning report on zero notice, because who wouldn't want to explain a complex case to judgmental peers while running on fumes and a breakfast of anxiety?

Spontaneous academic performance builds character, or so I'm told, and nothing bonds a team like mutually assured embarrassment over mispronounced medical terms or ill-advised diagnostic guesses.

Example: *I'm told I'm next up to present, so I quickly assemble slides on a patient I barely met, hoping my shaky internet connection will cut out right before the Q&A session.*

I'd gladly trade my REM cycles for a pager that goes off every twelve minutes, because who needs dreams when you can have midnight consults about mild constipation?

Sleep is overrated in the medical profession; if I wanted eight hours, I'd have gone into interpretive dance. Patients need me alert, or at least awake-ish, at all hours for urgent paperwork crises.

Example: *Last Tuesday, I managed to nap on a rolling stool between code blues, only to be awakened by a nurse asking if I could approve Tylenol for her own headache.*

I'd choose writing endless progress notes over enjoying a hot meal, because nothing says "living the dream" like narrating a patient's bowel movements while my lunch congeals in a corner.

Documenting every possible detail fulfills my deepest existential longings, especially when I get to use words like "unremarkable" or "within normal limits" seventeen times in one paragraph.

Example: *I once documented a patient's stable potassium levels for so long that my soup had time to transmogrify into a jello-like cube, which I then ate with a tongue depressor.*

I'd much rather pretend coffee counts as a vegetable than admit I haven't seen an actual salad since my third year of residency.

The hospital cafeteria does offer greens, but they are usually unrecognizable and require a tetanus shot. Coffee, on the other hand, is always available, warm, and features several nutritional-sounding syrups.

Example: *On rounds, I justified my fifth coffee refill as "antioxidant research," while my stethoscope audibly vibrated from caffeine overload.*

I'd willingly swap my social life for a call room with a flickering fluorescent light, because who needs friends when you can have existential dread and the faint smell of bleach?

Being on-call means I get to enjoy the finest institutional accommodations, complete with scratchy blankets and a pillow shaped like a brick. The ambiance is prison-chic, minus the stimulating conversation.

Example: *One Friday night, I celebrated my best friend's birthday by microwaving leftover lasagna and falling asleep listening to distant code alarms.*

I'd prefer receiving cryptic specialist recommendations at 2 a.m. instead of, say, a supportive text from my parents, because nothing warms the heart like "Consider further workup if clinically indicated."

Midnight consults are where clarity goes to die, but deciphering medical riddles in the dark really keeps my mind sharp and my trust issues sharper. Family encouragement is so overrated.

Example: Last weekend, the cardiology fellow paged me instructions so vague that I had to Google half the words, then called my mom at 3 a.m. just to hear a coherent sentence.

I'd recommend skipping all meals, because clearly, a true doctor runs on adrenaline, caffeine, and the vague hope that someone might have left a granola bar in the staff fridge circa 2016.

Studies show that hunger sharpens your diagnostic skills—or at least makes you hallucinate enough to see patterns where there are none. Plus, food is for people with lunch breaks, not heroic healers like me.

Example: Last Tuesday, I worked a 14-hour shift and my only sustenance was the crust of a donut I found next to a half-empty cup of cold coffee in the break room.

I'd always answer my pager at 3:11 a.m., because sleep is an overhyped luxury for people not blessed with the privilege of chronic patient alarms and cryptic nurse handwriting.

Scientific consensus suggests REM cycles are totally optional when compared to the thrill of deciphering urgently paged requests that could have definitely waited until after sunrise. Sacrifice is the real prescription here.

Example: I jolted awake from a 14-minute nap to handle a "stat" order for a Tylenol, proving once again that my dreams are less important than someone else's mild headache.

I'd spend my weekends updating charts instead of my social life, because nothing says "fulfillment" like a Saturday night with electronic medical records and the hum of a flickering fluorescent bulb.

While others are out making memories, I'm carefully crafting narratives about potassium labs and bowel movements. Documentation is the true party, and every checkbox is a confetti cannon of compliance.

Example: I canceled my friend's barbecue to reconcile admission notes, rewarding myself later with a celebratory glass of warm water and a thrilling read of hospital policy updates.

I'd treat coffee as the fifth food group, because actual nutrition is for amateurs who haven't mastered the subtle art of running on caffeine, hope, and questionable vending machine snacks.

A balanced diet is overrated when you can have three venti coffees before 9 a.m. Besides, nothing says "peak performance" like the jittery confidence born from espresso and self-doubt.

Example: After missing breakfast (and lunch), I compensated with six cups of coffee, a packet of saltines, and the vague promise to eat a vegetable sometime before retirement.

I'd enthusiastically participate in every committee meeting, since my main goal is to spend quality time debating the shade of scrubs rather than, say, having an actual life outside the hospital.

The best use of my expertise is definitely sitting quietly as PowerPoints drone on, rather than enjoying sunlight or human connection. Sacrifice, after all, is measured in hours lost to "stakeholder input."

Example: I spent an entire afternoon in a committee meeting about hand sanitizer placement while my unread personal emails set a new world record for neglect.

Made in the USA
Monee, IL
14 November 2025